WARNING:

Never insult an Indian within ten miles of
Little Big Horn.
—*General George Custer.*

The Official Book of Insults

Milt Rosen

PINNACLE BOOKS ◎ NEW YORK

I'd love to insult a duckbilled platypus, but how?

—*Charles Darwin.*

An original Pinnacle Books edition, published for the first time anywhere.

First printing, December 1983

ISBN: 0-523-42100-1

Can. ISBN: 0-523-43098-1

Cover illustration by Scott Ross

Printed in the United States of America

PINNACLE BOOKS, INC.
1430 Broadway
New York, New York 10018

9   8   7   6   5   4   3   2   1

Author's Foreword

The dawn of human time.

Primitive man, his stomach heavy with another charbroiled dinosaur steak, sits around the fire in his cave amid family and friends. Primitive man is not having the time of his life because he has not yet mastered the art of conversation. Whatever else they are, grunting and belching become boring after a while.

Primitive man's sister enters the cave. Primitive sister is obese, weighing in the neighborhood of a plump buffalo.

Primitive man smiles. "Primitive sister," he says, in one of those rare moments of inventiveness that change history, "you are fat. When you sit around the cave, you really sit around the cave."

There is laughter, then there is silence.

Eyes widen.

Hearts start to pound.

All gathered gulp.

A cheer forces its way through primitive lips.

Primitive man has just invented the insult. The art of conversation has found its tongue.

It's possible that primitive man could as easily have given birth to the compliment. Fortunately, in those primeval days there was little to compliment anyone about. Primitive man and woman were less than gorgeous. The closest thing to a compliment primitive man might have conjured up would doubtless have been something like, "For a fat broad you don't sweat too much." Hardly the figure of speech upon which to build an empire of dialogue. The path to insult was smoother.

Insults are more stimulating. They lower the mighty, wound the formidable, and, used properly, demonstrate how wonderfully vicious people can be. As Socrates said, "If you can't say something rotten about somebody, keep your mouth shut."

This volume is dedicated to those who march through life to the jarring drumbeats of insolence, rudeness, disrespect, brazenness, arrogance, disdain, impudence, incivility, rusticity, disparagement, and contumely.

Table of Insults

I

LOSER! DEADBEAT! JERK!

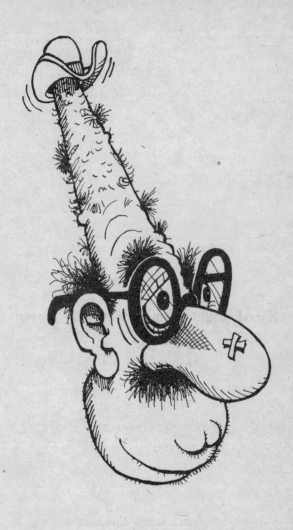

He has a point. It's his head.

She was so unpopular, she had to go to the senior prom with the security guard.

* * *

What's he doing here? Somebody close the poolroom?

* * *

People should play house with him. He could be the door and they'd slam him.

* * *

Nobody could warm up to him . . . even if they were being cremated together.

* * *

He's a fugitive from the law of averages.

* * *

Those who didn't know him said he was a bum. Those who knew him could swear to it.

He never did a thing in his life, and he didn't do that too well.

* * *

In a world of tuxedos, he's a brown shoe.

* * *

She's class conscious. She has no class and everybody's conscious.

* * *

She knows all the dirty words . . . dust, cook, wash.

* * *

He's a born deadbeat. If you sent him a bill that was a year old, he'd send you a birthday card.

* * *

Somebody get a plumber. There's a drip in here.

4

He has a strange hobby. He sits home and collects dust.

If baloney was snow, people still wouldn't get his drift.

* * *

Is he a self-made man or does somebody else have to take the rap?

* * *

He crossed in front of a black cat the other day and it's had bad luck ever since.

* * *

There are people you wouldn't give two cents for. His type is six for a nickel.

* * *

He had to get a job recently. He was too nervous to steal.

* * *

He went back to school recently to learn a trade, so he'd know what kind of work he was out of.

* * *

When she asks a man what he wants out of their relationship, he usually says . . . her.

6

This is the first pair of shoes I've seen with three heels.

* * *

They're a pair of baseball girls. They were thrown out at home.

* * *

He went to the dentist for an examination. His teeth are fine, but his gums will have to come out.

* * *

People want to pay him what he's worth, but he won't work that cheap.

* * *

He left his last job because of illness and fatigue. His boss got sick and tired of him.

* * *

He was an unwanted baby. They bought him sandpaper diapers.

* * *

He's a man of the first water . . . a drip.

He comes from a moneyed family. His brother is worth fifty thousand dollars, dead or alive.

* * *

He's not himself today. It looks as if he's got the best of the deal.

* * *

He wants people to have a good time, but he hangs around anyway.

* * *

He's so dull he couldn't even entertain a doubt.

* * *

He lights up a room by leaving it.

* * *

She feels like a new woman . . . and she should be.

* * *

For years he was an unknown failure. Now he's a known failure.

8

He gives failure a bad name.

* * *

He had a lot of get up and go, but unfortunately he didn't.

* * *

He's trying. In fact he's really trying.

* * *

He used to have the wolf at his door. Now he has no door.

* * *

He's so rotten, when he dies, instead of a will, he'll have a won't.

* * *

He has the makings of a perfect stranger.

* * *

If they ever put a price on his head, he should take it.

For a minute they didn't recognize him, and they never spent a more enjoyable moment.

* * *

He wouldn't tell his girl he wasn't good enough for her. He wanted it to come as a surprise.

* * *

If it wasn't for her dress, people would never recognize her.

* * *

He's a self-made mouse.

* * *

He made a fool of himself. You can tell he's a perfect craftsman.

* * *

He's got a terrible inferiority complex and he's perfectly right.

* * *

He was a pen pal. That's where he wrote from.

If he had his life to live over, he still wouldn't be sure he did it the first time.

* * *

He's so unpopular he only got into the dating service through a blind date.

* * *

He felt inferior, so he went to a psychiatrist to become more positive. Now he's positive he's inferior.

* * *

She was stood up at the Father-Daughter Dance.

* * *

She's the salt of the earth. People keep trying to shake her.

* * *

The other day she was in a place for the first time—her kitchen.

* * *

Men tell her that her hair is like a mop. She doesn't mind. She doesn't know what a mop is.

He's so frightened, when he makes love he wears a seat belt.

* * *

He keeps complaining that his virility is too high. It's in his mind.

* * *

His picture is in the dictionary, under "mediocre."

* * *

He outsmarted the recession of the 80's. He stopped working in the 70's.

* * *

If Hite had known about him, she would have had another Report.

* * *

Men like him are very rare. They should be well-done.

* * *

He comes from Akron, the rubber city. It's a shame his father never used one.

He bought a stock at twenty. It went down thirty points.

* * *

She can't type too well, but she can erase fifty words a minute.

* * *

He loves three things—women, money, and both.

* * *

She doesn't go in for group sex. She wouldn't know whom to thank.

* * *

He has no luck. Last week his swimming pool burned down.

* * *

He tried to make a name for himself. He's a forger.

* * *

People give her a constipated greeting. They say hello but they don't give a shit.

He doesn't even walk in his sleep. He hitchhikes.

* * *

He hates to get up in the morning. It keeps him awake the rest of the day.

* * *

He's very familiar with hard work. He's fought it successfully for years.

* * *

He gets into a stew faster than an oyster.

* * *

He has been compared to many of his friends . . . and quite unfavorably.

* * *

He started out working for peanuts until he could prove his salt. Now he has salted peanuts.

* * *

He's a miracle worker. It's a miracle when he works.

He really has no luck. His artificial flowers died.

* * *

He's part of the new metallic age—gold in his teeth, silver in his hair, and lead in his pants.

* * *

She was two-thirds married once. She and the preacher were there.

* * *

His business is looking up. It's flat on its back.

* * *

It wouldn't do him any good to see himself as others see him. He wouldn't believe it.

* * *

He got his stoop living up to his ideals.

* * *

He would have cooked his goose a long time ago but he didn't have a pot.

He could be the poster boy for vasecto-
mies.

He was so busy learning the tricks of the trade he forgot to learn the trade.

* * *

She has no class. For her, soap on a rope is jewelry.

* * *

He should be a good swimmer. He's been up the creek for years.

* * *

He keeps running into accidents that start out happening to someone else.

* * *

When he started out, he didn't have a nickel in his pocket. Now after thirty years of hard work, he has a nickel in his pocket.

* * *

He worked as a mattress tester, but one day he fell awake on the job.

* * *

He's working his way down from the bottom.

He used to work in a vineyard, stomping grapes with his feet. But he got fired. They found him sitting down on the job.

18

There's a man who was born at the bottom and stayed there.

* * *

He leads a dog's life. He comes into the house tracking mud, warms himself by the fire, and waits to be fed.

* * *

He's so unpopular, the FBI put him on its unwanted list.

* * *

He has no luck. He once got the clap from a toilet seat at the Vatican.

* * *

He's as useful as a glass eye at a keyhole.

* * *

He wanted to join a nudist colony, but he didn't have the balls for it.

* * *

He needs two desks . . . one for each foot.

His gambling brought his family together. He lost their house and they had to move into one room.

* * *

She's been turned down so often, she looks like a bedspread.

* * *

His parents spent ten years trying to find a loophole in his birth certificate.

* * *

He's done a lot for the human race. He's not in it.

* * *

For years he wondered about what was the secret of his success. Then he discovered he wasn't a success.

* * *

His get up and go got up and went.

* * *

He thinks the world owes him a giving.

He looks like the poster boy for birth control.

* * *

He must get awfully tired of having himself around.

* * *

Whenever he feels like doing anything he lies down on the couch till the desire passes.

* * *

He's on his back so much he hasn't seen his shadow in years.

* * *

He's very busy with the stock market . . . He has a seat on the curb.

* * *

He believes in the hereafter. He's here after a meal, a loan . . .

* * *

He doesn't care which side his bread is buttered on. He says that he eats both sides.

His family has always served the country . . . some of them ten years, some life.

* * *

He comes from an alert family. His uncle was the lookout at Pearl Harbor.

* * *

Most people feel like his proctologist. They've seen enough of that asshole.

* * *

She doesn't know if she's pregnant or not. The rabbit's in a coma.

* * *

He wears a rubber when he makes love. The dampness is bad for his arthritis.

* * *

The only time he can hear anything good about himself is when he talks to himself.

* * *

His wife doesn't know how tall he is. It's been years since she saw him standing up.

He was a real worm. He came along, wiggled a little, and some chicken got him.

* * *

One girl kept trying to break down his door. He had locked her in his room.

* * *

He became a father recently. They must have lowered the requirements.

* * *

He prefers masturbation to regular sex because he doesn't have to get up in the middle of the night to drive his hand home.

* * *

He puts off until tomorrow everything he's already put off until today.

* * *

A day away from him is like a month in the country.

* * *

He has the first dollar he ever earned. But he only got it yesterday.

He's so unpopular, they had to tie a pork chop around his neck so his dog would play with him.

She always makes something delicious for dinner . . . reservations.

* * *

He doesn't know when he's well-off because he never is.

* * *

He has to ask permission to ask permission.

* * *

If he disappears suddenly, it couldn't happen to a nicer guy.

* * *

She's an exception to the law of gravity. It's easier to pick her up than to drop her.

* * *

His back goes out more often than he does.

* * *

His mother loved children. She would have given anything if he'd been one.

He's very lazy. He gets into a revolving door and waits.

* * *

He was the teacher's pet. She couldn't afford a dog.

* * *

He's the kind of guy who'd take a cab to bankruptcy court and then invite the cabbie in as another creditor.

* * *

You have to give him a lot of credit. He has no cash.

* * *

He was an awkward kid. If he fell in a barrel of tits, he'd come up sucking his thumb.

* * *

He loves animals. He gives half his money to the horses.

* * *

The only thing that lies more than he does is falsies.

He works all the time. He's a picket.

* * *

He does nothing all day, and by ten at night he's half through.

* * *

He has a fantastic labor-saving device. He calls it "tomorrow."

* * *

He has terrible insomnia. He keeps waking up every few days.

* * *

He does most of his work sitting down. That's where he shines.

* * *

He was dangerously ill for a while. Now he's dangerously well.

* * *

She just got a part-time job in a department store. Three nights a week she's a guard dog.

He's not in bad shape. It's just that the parts of his body don't want to work together anymore.

* * *

He's as important as a VD doctor in a senior citizens' home.

II

OLD!
(BOY, WHAT A
FOSSIL!)

Her age is a military secret. The Civil War.

* * *

She doesn't show her age but if you look under her makeup it's there.

* * *

People who knew her thirty years ago say she still looks as she did then . . .old.

* * *

He's at the age where the only thing that gets steamed up is his glasses.

* * *

She will never be as old as she looks.

* * *

She doesn't need a necklace. She just braids her wrinkles.

* * *

She doesn't make up her face. She assembles it.

She finally reached middle age . . . for the fourth time.

* * *

He's getting old. It takes him half the time to get tired and twice the time to get rested.

* * *

- They gave her something for her gray hair. Respect.

* * *

He has baseball eyes—two-baggers.

* * *

He was a tightrope walker, but he got fired. He was always tighter than the rope.

* * *

She was born in the Year of Our Lord only knows.

* * *

By the time she finished lighting the last candle on her birthday. cake, the first one had gone out.

Most people are here today and gone tomorrow. He's here today and he's here tomorrow.

* * *

Her last birthday cake looked like a prairie fire.

* * *

If they put his real age on his birthday cake, it would be a fire hazard.

* * *

The last time she lit the candles on her birthday cake, she barbecued the ceiling.

* * *

Thirty is a nice age for a woman, especially if she's fifty.

* * *

She's pretty old. Her social security number is 2.

* * *

She just turned thirty-five, a real U-turn.

He may be getting old but he's still in there pinching.

* * *

He still chases women but he can't remember why.

* * *

He had so many wrinkles on his forehead he had to screw on his hat.

* * *

He's real optimist. He's eighty-four and he's looking for a home near a school.

* * *

His head makes dates that his body has trouble keeping.

* * *

He dines with the upper set. He should use the lowers too.

* * *

She was named after Betsy Ross . . . and not long after.

Her hair was so gray she had to buy Grecian Formula 32.

* * *

Nobody lives forever, but she's trying.

* * *

She gets her hair done in a place that picks up and delivers.

* * *

She knew Howard Johnson when he only had two flavors.

* * *

The ancient Greeks had a word for it . . . and she was there to hear it.

* * *

He's at the age where all the numbers in his little black book are doctors.

* * *

He keeps her picture on his desk, but he doesn't remember why.

If he had his life to live over, he shouldn't.

* * *

She's discovered the secret of eternal youth. She lies about her age.

* * *

She found the fountain of youth. It's called a plastic surgeon.

* * *

She's been pressing thirty so long, it's pleated.

* * *

You can tell she's twenty-eight. Just count the rings under her eyes.

* * *

When he was a kid, he lived in a tenement with only one bathroom on each floor. He swore he'd grow up, become rich, build a house, and have ten bathrooms. He grew up, became rich, built a house, and has ten bathrooms. Now he can't go.

The bags under her eyes are so big, she needs a porter to get out of bed in the morning.

* * *

It's not that she has bags under her eyes. It's that her bags have bags.

III

CHEAP!
TIGHTWAD!

He was born with a silver spoon in his mouth, and every time he goes into a restaurant, he tries to complete the set.

* * *

He's pretty snappy, just like his checks.

* * *

He's so cheap, he saves money by eating his heart out.

* * *

He's so tight, when he winks his kneecaps move.

* * *

He's the kind of guy who hates a nickel because it isn't a dime.

* * *

He gives no quarter. For that matter he doesn't tip dimes either.

* * *

He's very charitable. When the Home For the Aged asked for a donation, he gave them his mother and father.

When there's a call for charity, he puts his hand in his pocket right away . . . and leaves it there.

* * *

The man is a lady-killer. He starves his dates to death.

* * *

He gives the Lord credit for everything. It's a shame that when he goes to church he doesn't give Him some cash.

* * *

He's made an art of avoiding picking up checks. You have to hand it to him.

* * *

His drink must be sick, he's been nursing it for an hour.

* * *

He's the carefree type. He doesn't care as long as it's free.

His outfit is real cheap. Yesterday it shrank two inches and it was only cloudy outside.

* * *

He keeps divorcing ugly wives. It's cheaper than sending them to the beauty parlor.

* * *

He's cheap. He doesn't get a haircut every four weeks, he just gets his ears lowered.

* * *

He thinks nothing is too good for her . . . and that's what he gives her—nothing.

* * *

He's a real cheapskate. He just bought his wife a fifty-piece dinner set: a box of toothpicks.

* * *

Money goes through his fingers like glue.

* * *

She wanted a foreign convertible . . . so he bought her a rickshaw.

He's so cheap, he hypnotized his wife into thinking she was a canary so she'd eat birdseed. He went even further then. He hypnotized her into thinking she was a sparrow, so she'd go out and find her own food.

* * *

He wants to die with his boots on. He's got holes in his socks.

* * *

His drinks are so weak they won't even stain the tablecloth.

* * *

He's always trying to pass the buck, except when it has Washington's picture on it.

* * *

He's so tight he won't even tip his hat.

* * *

He's a big spender. He orders asparagus and leaves the waiter the tips.

He's a man of rare gifts. He hasn't given one in years.

* * *

He's so cheap, he keeps his wife's teeth with him to keep her from eating between meals.

* * *

He never gives her money for the table. How much can a table eat?

* * *

You can always spot him at a dinner party. He sits with his back to the check.

* * *

He's got low pockets and short arms.

* * *

He'd give you the sleeves off his vest.

* * *

At dinner he sits as if the check is going to reach out and grab him.

He never gave her a present, but he did give her a pretty good past.

* * *

He throws money around like a man without arms.

* * *

He borrows so much his will is made out to the small claims court.

IV

LOUDMOUTH!

She claims to be outspoken, but she's hardly ever.

* * *

He not only holds a conversation, he strangles it.

* * *

He has foot-in-the-mouth disease.

* * *

Everything you tell her goes in one ear and over the phone.

* * *

When he says he wants to make a long story short, it's already too late.

* * *

He always walks into a room voice first.

* * *

Speaking of speaking, she's generally speaking.

She went to the beach and talked so much she ended up with a smoked tongue.

* * *

He's getting a little tired. You can tell because he can hardly keep his mouth open.

* * *

He never knows what they're arguing about. She won't tell him.

* * *

He found a way of keeping the inside of his car quiet. It fits right over her mouth.

* * *

He just came back from a pleasure trip. He took his wife to the airport.

* * *

Her tongue is her greatest weapon. It should be a secret one.

* * *

She's an amazon—big at the mouth.

He's a man of few words, but he keeps repeating them.

* * *

He always opens something by mistake . . . his mouth.

* * *

His wife is a politician—the speaker of the house.

* * *

He shoots his mouth off so much he brushes his teeth with gunpowder.

* * *

After everything is said and done, he just keeps on talking.

* * *

She's a real complainer. Gold is the only thing she hasn't panned.

* * *

He reads her like a book. Too bad he can't shut her up the same way.

His mouth is so big he can whisper in his own ear.

* * *

Her vocabulary is limited in words, but what a turnover!

* * *

You couldn't get a word in with her even if you folded it in two.

* * *

They're always having words . . . hers.

* * *

She doesn't like to repeat gossip, but what else can she do with it.

* * *

He has to remember to keep his mouth closed. He's catching flies.

* * *

She's good at making things—like mountains out of molehills.

He never opens his mouth unless he has nothing to say.

* * *

Her mind is always on the tip of her tongue.

* * *

She used to look like a siren. Now she sounds like one.

* * *

She's got a keen sense of rumor.

* * *

He has a problem. He has to feed eight small mouths . . . and listen to one big one.

* * *

When his wife said that she was outspoken, he gulped and asked, "By whom?"

Her tongue is so big she can lick an envelope after it's in the mailbox.

* * *

He recently acquired a huge vocabulary. He married it.

* * *

She was sent from heaven just for him. They must like quiet up there.

* * *

She used to be tongue-tied. Now it moves so fast nobody can grab it to tie a knot in it.

V

UG-LY!
BOW WOW!
ECCH!

His father was an electrician and he was his first shock.

* * *

When time marched on, it must have stepped on his face.

* * *

When she was born they didn't know whether to buy a crib or a cage.

* * *

He looks so ugly, people think his neck barfed.

* * *

She can't be two-faced or she'd be using the other one.

* * *

He must be a baker, he has such a bun on.

* * *

She had her face lifted. Who would want to steal a thing like that?

There are a lot of fish in the ocean, but she looks like the bait.

She has a great head on her shoulders. Too bad it's not on her neck.

* * *

Why didn't he let the undertaker finish the job on him?

* * *

I'm glad to see your back, especially after seeing your face.

* * *

The plastic surgeon wouldn't give her a boob uplift because there'd be nothing left in her shoes.

* * *

Her face proves that love is blind.

* * *

She has the kind of face you want to tune-in a little clearer.

* * *

She's so ugly, men look at her and dress her with their eyes.

He's had it rough lately. His organ grinder
died.

We've all seen better looking pans in hospital beds.

* * *

She got her nose from her father. He's a plastic surgeon.

* * *

They didn't use silicone on her. They used silly putty.

* * *

Her silicone was probably mixed with hamburger helper.

* * *

He has the kind of face that could pose for cab driver pictures.

* * *

The other day she was crying. A tear rolled down her cheek, took a look at her face, and rolled right up again.

* * *

He was a war baby. His folks took one look at him and started fighting.

The last time anybody saw a head like that it was on a bag of oats.

* * *

There was something strange about her eyes. One was green and the other two were blue.

* * *

They used to call her "Baby." She had one tooth.

* * *

He'd give a riveter the jitters.

* * *

He wants to know what's going to happen to him. It looks as if it already did.

* * *

He doesn't have any enemies but his friends won't be seen with him.

* * *

When she was born, the doctor took one look and *he* went into the recovery room.

She has the looks that turn heads . . .
and stomachs.

* * *

She had a far away look about her. Far
away she didn't look bad.

* * *

She's so hairy, her knees have bangs.

* * *

She's so hairy, she doesn't need a coat. She
is a coat.

* * *

She looks as if she just stepped out of
Vogue and fell flat on her face.

* * *

She had a nose that would look silly on an
anteater.

* * *

She was such an ugly bride, everybody
got in line to kiss the caterer.

If she was nude she could model for Milk
Duds.

*   *   *

If all women are sisters under the skin,
why doesn't she get back under the skin and
send out her sister?

*   *   *

His shirts had ring around the collar, and
there was one through his nose.

*   *   *

Her family went back to the Dark Ages.
She kept up the tradition because she was a
sight in the light.

*   *   *

She has a pretty little head. For a head it's
pretty little.

*   *   *

If God had seen her, he would have made
another Commandment.

61

When she was a kid her mother had to buy
her back from the dog catcher twice a week.

It's a shame his parents didn't have any children.

* * *

Her boyfriend must be an archeologist. He seems to like ruins.

* * *

People knock everything about her except her knees. Nature beat them to that.

* * *

He was recently arrested for sodomy, and he was alone at the time.

* * *

She has Brooke Shields' body, only she's had it forty-five years longer.

* * *

Her canary flies around the house with its wings over its eyes.

* * *

Men don't bother her. She wishes they would.

He was at Harvard Medical School for three years . . . as an exhibit.

She finally showed her true colors. She ran out of makeup.

* * *

She reminds people of an Indian expression—Ugh!

* * *

It was love at first sight. Unfortunately, he took another look.

* * *

Is that a girl? Is that a girl? That's what everybody keeps asking—Is that a girl?

* * *

She has a face like a flower . . . cauliflower.

* * *

Didn't we meet at the morgue, when they opened your drawer?

Is that a girl? Is that a girl? You can answer "yes" or "no" and still not be right.

* * *

He can overlook anything . . . except his nose.

* * *

They should have named her Estée Lauder. She belongs in a jar.

* * *

She went skydiving and her chute didn't open. But she didn't get hurt. She landed on her makeup.

* * *

His head looks like one continuous face.

* * *

He loves nature, which is very nice of him considering what nature did to him.

* * *

People shouldn't make cracks about her face. It has enough without any help.

They ought to call her Flour because she's been through the mill.

* * *

She walked into a bar one time. Seven men took the pledge.

* * *

He looks like an accident waiting to happen.

* * *

She has so many cavities in her teeth, she has to talk through her neckline.

* * *

Her face looks as if it's worn out six bodies.

* * *

It's easy to get rid of her. Just hold up a cross.

* * *

She's very religious. People look at her and say, "Oh, God."

He looks like he's ready to grab somebody, climb the Empire State Building, and wait to get shot down by an airplane.

68

She got a dress for a ridiculous figure—hers.

* * *

She sent her picture to the Lonely Hearts Club. It was sent back with the explanation that they were lonely, not desperate.

* * *

Nobody comes to her house anymore. She keeps biting people on the ankle.

* * *

She has a schoolgirl complexion, except it looks as if it was expelled.

* * *

The other day she ran into the grim reaper. That's her hair stylist.

* * *

She has beautiful long black hair . . . under her arms.

* * *

People meet him in nightmares.

69

She looks like a professional blind date.

* * *

She looked just like a mermaid, except the top half was a fish.

* * *

He looks like something the cat dragged in. She looks like the cat.

* * *

She has the kind of face that grows on you . . . if you're an ape.

* * *

He takes her everywhere he goes. It's easier than kissing her goodbye.

* * *

Hers is a peculiar shape for a woman . . . or a man . . . or a horse.

* * *

We've all seen better looking pans under ice boxes.

The stork who delivered him flew back-
wards so it wouldn't have to look at his face.

When he was born, his father went down
to the zoo and threw rocks at the stork.

They call her Bunny. She has a harelip.

* * *

Her face looks as if it rode on the rim for ten miles.

* * *

She once broke out in hives. She never looked better.

* * *

She has a wonderful way of protecting herself from Peeping Toms. She sleeps with the shades up.

* * *

A Peeping Tom looked in her window and turned himself in to the police.

VI

STUPID!

He'd have to step out of his mind to get an idea.

* * *

He has a brain, but it hasn't reached his head yet.

* * *

He'll never be too old to learn new ways of being stupid.

* * *

He asked her to marry him. She told him to ask her father, but he didn't. Her father didn't appeal to him.

* * *

He's the flower of youth—a blooming idiot!

* * *

He went to a mind reader once and got in for half-price.

* * *

They finally told him about the birds and the bees, but it's not doing him any good. He doesn't know any birds or bees.

Anybody can get lost in a fog, but he makes his own.

* * *

He's so dumb he doesn't carry a pocket comb. He says he never has to comb his pockets.

* * *

He's very cautious. He allows his kids to watch a solar eclipse but he warns them about standing too close.

* * *

He was once given the key to the city. The next day he locked himself out.

* * *

He sleeps at the edge of his bed so he can drop right off.

* * *

She told him that she wanted to see some change in him, so he swallowed some coins.

He changed his mind the other day. Too bad it doesn't work any better than the old one.

* * *

If he says he's got a cold or something in his head, it's a cold.

* * *

She's got a terrific stairway but there's not much upstairs.

* * *

He'd dip his finger in a glass to make sure he's got a soft drink.

* * *

He always stops to think. The trouble is he forgets to start up again.

* * *

The closest he'll ever come to a brain-storm is a slight drizzle.

She was hurt while taking a milk bath.
The cow fell on her.

He had panty hose tattooed on his stomach because he'd always wanted a chest of drawers.

* * *

He'd take his car out in a rainstorm because it was a driving rain.

* * *

When they told him about the birds and the bees he went to the park and gave head to a pigeon.

* * *

He was once arrested for taking his clothes off in front of a blind girl.

* * *

He's got an open mind, but it's really vacant.

* * *

He has brain damage. He was hit on the head by a falling napkin.

* * *

He should stick his head out of the window . . . feet first.

He's very naive. His wife gives him a tangerine and tells him he's having sex.

* * *

He once got a job as a pharmacist, but he was fired. He always broke the bottles in the typewriter.

* * *

He's so dumb he could freeze to death standing in front of a brothel's red light waiting for it to change.

* * *

The other day he had a bright idea . . . beginner's luck.

* * *

She's very naive. They asked her if she knew the baby's formula. She said, "Sure. Two hickeys and we turned out the light."

* * *

He has the brain of an idiot. He ought to give it back.

He fell out of his crib when he was a baby, but he was lucky. He broke the fall with his head.

Reincarnation must exist. Nobody could become as stupid as he in one lifetime.

* * *

When they were giving out brains, he was in another line getting a second helping of mouth.

* * *

People should be nice to him. He was kicked in the head by a butterfly.

* * *

If he was studying to be an idiot he'd flunk.

* * *

He has an open mind . . . a hole in his head.

* * *

His head should feel as good as new. He's never used it.

* * *

He should get a coffin to fit his shoulders. He's dead from the neck up.

Everybody has heard of flying saucers. He makes the cups for them.

* * *

With him it's not the heat, it's the stupidity.

* * *

When it comes to making people like him, he has a fat chance. And a head to match.

* * *

He has a soundproof head.

* * *

He was pretty dumb. He was sixteen before he knew he was fourteen.

* * *

He grew up in a tough neighborhood. It was fists, fists, fists for everything. He was fourteen before he knew he had fingers.

* * *

He'd like to give somebody a piece of his mind, but it's not big enough to divide.

He ought to blow his brains out. He has nothing to lose.

* * *

He ought to send his wits out to be sharpened.

* * *

Somebody ought to tell him he's a vacant room so he'd make himself scarce.

* * *

People think he's a wit. They're only half right.

* * *

He had more brains in his head than he had in his little finger . . . but not much more.

* * *

He makes up in stupidity what he lacks in personality.

* * *

He's pretty stupid. He wanted to buy his girlfriend lipstick, but he didn't know the size of her lips.

They named a town in New England after him—Marblehead.

* * *

When he gets an idea in his head it's a stowaway.

VII

DRUNK!

His eyes are pretty bloodshot. If he doesn't close them he'll bleed to death.

* * *

If you think his eyes are bloodshot, you should see them from the inside.

* * *

He ought to go to the blood bank and get his eyes drained.

* * *

After the first drink he feels like himself. After the second, he feels like a new man. After the third, he feels like a baby. He crawls all the way home.

* * *

He was down on liquor. He downed more than anybody else.

* * *

He spends a staggering amount on booze.

* * *

They call him a creep because that's how he gets home at night.

Nobody knew she drank until one day they saw her sober.

* * *

They say he's a hard drinker. Actually it's the easiest thing he does.

* * *

He drinks to calm himself down. Last week he got so calm he couldn't move.

* * *

He has great respect for old age, especially if it's bottled.

* * *

He's a real boozer. He thinks of any apartment with more than one bath as a distillery.

* * *

He drinks a lot. When somebody asks him if he wants beer, scotch, gin, or vodka, he says, "Yes."

He ruined his health drinking to everybody else's.

* * *

Every morning he gets up tight and early.

* * *

She spent so much time drinking, her
teeth were bottle-capped.

* * *

He ought to learn that it's okay to drink
like a fish . . . if you drink what a fish
drinks.

* * *

He's been thrown out of so many places,
he's got ties to match the sidewalk.

* * *

She doesn't wear glasses. She just emp-
ties them.

* * *

She doesn't have to wear glasses to make
a spectacle of herself.

90

About an hour ago he was sitting on the curb trying to get his mind out of the gutter.

* * *

She's so high most of the time she gets spirit messages.

* * *

He saw a sign that said, "Drink Canada Dry." He went.

* * *

When the dt's get drunk they see him.

* * *

She drinks so much, every time you dance with her you can hear her slosh.

* * *

He took a blood test once and it came back marked "Smirnoff."

* * *

If you took one look at him you wouldn't think he was drunk. You'd think he was dead.

You don't realize he's loaded until he shoots his mouth off.

* * *

He's leaned on so many bars his clothes have padded elbows.

* * *

He comes from lush country—a country full of lushes.

* * *

The hardest thing he learned in college was to open beer bottles with a quarter.

* * *

Women like him because he's tall, dark, and had some.

* * *

He only drinks at certain times during the day—morning, noon, four, five . . .

* * *

Nobody makes him drink the way he does. He's a volunteer.

He wore sunglasses to protect his eyes from the glare of his nose.

* * *

They're a nice match. They're both always lit.

* * *

She never drinks unless she's alone or with somebody.

* * *

One day he got drunk and ended up in the zebra's cage at the zoo. He got no sleep at all. He spent the whole night trying to take off her pajamas.

* * *

She must be Mary, Queen of Scotch.

* * *

He believes there's no place like home. After all, the other places close.

* * *

He drinks to forget he drinks.

He drinks quite a bit. Last week he fell down twice under his own power.

* * *

She can't swim a stroke but she knows every dive in town.

VIII

HOLY
DEADLOCK . . .
ER, WEDLOCK.

He's not always a yesman. When his wife says "No" he says "No."

* * *

They have a lot of children. She's trying to lose him in the crowd.

* * *

He never gets up with a grouch. He gets out of bed before she does.

* * *

He married her for her looks but not the kind he's getting now.

* * *

She picks his clothes. She starts with his pockets.

* * *

He wears the pants in his house . . . under his apron.

* * *

When an application asks him his marital status, he writes "Below wife."

When he gets a contented look on his face she wipes it off with a dish towel.

* * *

She was a sleepy bride. She couldn't stay awake for a second.

* * *

When they started to go together she listened. They got married and he listened. Now after ten years, the neighbors listen.

* * *

Their marriage was like a bathtub. Once he got in it wasn't so hot.

* * *

She's his bitter half.

* * *

She wants him to buy her a harness. If she works like a horse she wants to look like a horse.

* * *

She spent the first part of her life looking for a husband. Now she's spending the second part wondering where he is.

She can't go home to her mother because her mother still lives with her mother.

* * *

Ten years ago they were joined in holy deadlock.

* * *

He never takes her anywhere at night. All he takes out at night now is his teeth.

* * *

She's got something that'll knock your eyes out—a jealous husband.

* * *

When his wife died he married her sister so he wouldn't have to break in a new mother-in-law.

* * *

He found something to settle his wife's hash . . . Rolaids!

* * *

He misses his wife's cooking . . . every chance he gets.

He says grace at the dinner table but his wife objects to him talking about her in his sleep.

* * *

He's been married thirty years and it seems like only yesterday. And everybody knows what a miserable day yesterday was.

* * *

She had given him the best years of her life . . . 1976, 1979, and two months in 1980.

* * *

His wife has him eating out of her hand. She hates to do the dishes.

* * *

He always gets homesick—that's why he leaves it.

* * *

He keeps wishing his wife was his mother so he could run away from home.

He's a very lucky man. He has a wife and a lighter and they both work.

* * *

They have a great marriage. He brings home the bacon and she burns it.

* * *

When his wife's doctor told him that his wife needed sex a dozen times a month, he volunteered for two of them.

* * *

He doesn't have sex with his wife anymore. He uses jumper cables.

* * *

One day he brought home fifty pounds of ice. His wife cooked it and drowned.

* * *

He keeps his teeth in great condition. He never argues with her.

* * *

They ought to call her husband Henry. He's the eighth.

Her husband never makes love to her. If he didn't toss and turn in his sleep they wouldn't have any kids.

* * *

She left her husband cold. She buried him.

* * *

She's a great housekeeper. After the divorce she always keeps it.

* * *

When they met, he proposed to her and he said he would die for her. Unfortunately, he hasn't.

* * *

His wife wants to be something she's never been . . . a widow.

* * *

One marriage in four ends in a divorce. They're fighting it to a finish.

* * *

He's a confirmed bachelor. He figures if it was good enough for his father it's good enough for him.

He doesn't want to set the world on fire . . . just his wife.

* * *

He used to read her like a book. Now he just thumbs through the pages once in a while.

* * *

One day a thief stole all her credit cards. Her husband didn't report it. The thief was spending less than she was.

* * *

They never considered getting a divorce. Neither of them wanted the kids.

* * *

When he married her he said that her hands would never touch dishwater, and he kept his promise. He bought her rubber gloves.

* * *

When she walks down the aisle she takes the groom's arm because she knows the way better than he does.

A lot of people fought for her hand. Her husband lost.

* * *

When her husband married her, he could have eaten her alive. Now he's sorry he didn't.

* * *

She got a divorce because her husband was careless about his appearance. He didn't show up for two years.

* * *

He always called himself a bachelor. Then he got married. Now people blush when they hear what he calls himself.

* * *

They divide the chores around the house. He washes the dishes and she sweeps them up.

* * *

He's her new husband, but he's not a working model.

When a wife runs off, it's always with the husband's best friend, even if the husband doesn't know the guy.

* * *

When she got married she wasn't happy . . . just triumphant.

* * *

She didn't want to marry him for his money, but that was the only way she could get it.

* * *

She's unmarried . . . occasionally.

* * *

His wedding ring was like a tourniquet. It stopped his circulation.

* * *

Jews don't get divorces. They figure they've had five thousand years of persecution so what's one marriage.

* * *

She used to be his secretary. Then they got married and now *he* takes dictation.

They're always holding hands. If they'd let go they'd kill each other.

* * *

They were recently separated. She went home to her mother and he went home to his wife.

* * *

She's compulsively neat. If he gets up at three in the morning for a drink of water, when he comes back the bed is made.

* * *

She married him for life, but until now he hasn't shown any.

* * *

On his wedding night he told his wife they were seeing too much of each other.

* * *

When he gets up in the morning, he says "I'm sorry" to his wife, and that covers him for the whole day.

He's had trouble with two wives—the first one left him and the second one won't.

* * *

He didn't mind his wife eating crackers in bed until one night he came home and found a crumb in the closet.

* * *

He knows when they're going to have a salad for dinner. He doesn't smell anything burning.

* * *

He wants her to live in the manner to which she's been accustomed, so he's letting her keep her job.

* * *

Not long ago a tornado blew them out of their house. It was the first time in years they went anywhere together.

* * *

She gives him too much rope . . . which is why he's always tied up with his secretary.

He gave his girlfriend a mink coat to keep her warm. Then he gave one to his wife to keep her cool.

* * *

He's a second-story man. His wife never believes his first one.

* * *

They're inseparable at night. It takes three cops to pull them apart.

* * *

They fight like two halves of an Alka Seltzer.

* * *

He can never forget their wedding. He tries to but his wife won't let him.

* * *

He envies only one man . . . his wife's first husband.

* * *

They can never forget the first time they met, but they both keep trying.

Her body gives him a problem. She wants it covered with a fur coat.

*   *   *

A year after they were married there was the pitter-patter of tiny feet around the house. Her parents were midgets.

*   *   *

He told her to go to the devil, so she went home to her mother.

*   *   *

They have a beautiful apartment overlooking the rent.

*   *   *

It's true that two can live cheaper than one, but it's worth the difference to stay single.

*   *   *

They've been married for ten years and he still talks in his sleep. He doesn't want to forget how.

He thinks nothing is too good for her . . . and so does she.

* * *

Tonight's the night he gets his annual hard-on. It's also the night his wife gets her annual headache.

* * *

They're like a movie: *Star Bores*.

* * *

She's been to the altar so often she's been ordained.

* * *

He tried to get a car for his wife, but nobody would swap him.

* * *

The morning after their honeymoon she made burnt toast, gummy coffee, and dried eggs. That's when he realized she couldn't *cook* either.

* * *

She's a dedicated wife. She hasn't left his wallet in ten years.

He's been married eight times . . . and he's gonna keep at it until he gets it right.

* * *

She's the jealous type. At her wedding she had male bridesmaids.

IX

SEX FIEND!

In school she was chosen as the girl most likely to.

* * *

She must be with the Secret Service. She spends all her time undercover.

* * *

She's a homebody. Anybody's home.

* * *

He lives on the wrong side of a one-track mind.

* * *

All he thinks of is women. In fact, he's got a one-track mind. But what scenery along that track!

* * *

He has a one-track mind . . . a dirty track.

* * *

She's so oversexed, her knees haven't met in years.

She named her first baby after the father . . . "Army."

* * *

In her case, they're charging the stork with something that should be blamed on a lark.

* * *

What fattened her up didn't come off a plate.

* * *

He comes from a sexy family. His grandfather died at the age of one hundred and five. He was shot by a jealous husband.

* * *

He's a great lawyer. He once had a parking ticket reduced to manslaughter.

* * *

When you go out with her, it's cafeteria-style. You help yourself.

* * *

She's trying to find herself, but she picks the weirdest places to look.

She fools around so much, each knee thinks it's the only one.

* * *

They think she has a clear conscience. Actually it's just a poor memory.

* * *

She spent four years in a house of ill repute and had a nervous breakdown. She found out the other girls were getting paid.

* * *

She didn't know where her husband spent his evenings. One night she came home and there he was.

* * *

He was once arrested for statutory rape. He swore he didn't know she was a statue.

* * *

He was once arrested for sodomy, but plea-bargained his way down to "following too close."

One night a week he goes out with the boys. The other six *she* goes out with them.

* * *

It's easy to explain their baby. His car stalled and she didn't.

* * *

She shows everything but good taste.

* * *

His girl knows which came first—the bird or the egg . . . because she got them both.

* * *

She's so horny, she has landing lights on her stomach.

* * *

She drives a conversible. Everyone's talking about how she got it.

* * *

She has boyfriends by the score . . . and most of them do.

The only way she could keep out of trouble is if she glued her pants on.

* * *

Why do people say she's a wild girl? Almost anybody can pet her.

* * *

She's a regular soft-drink girl. She goes with anybody from 7-Up.

* * *

She's so oversexed, her rape whistle plays Johnny Mathis ballads.

* * *

He's a wolf in cheap clothing.

* * *

She was wearing only a beautiful fur coat, and he spent the entire date trying to get under her skin.

She sowed her wild oats and then prayed for a crop failure.

* * *

He was arrested for having sex with an ostrich. He said that if he knew they were going to make such a fuss he would have married her.

* * *

She treats him like dirt. She always hides him under her bed.

* * *

She believes that to err is human, but it feels divine.

* * *

She never tells him when she's having a climax. He's never around.

* * *

He often accuses her of infidelity but she swears she's been faithful to him many times.

The poor guy can't keep his wife in clothes. He bought her a house and can't keep her in that either.

* * *

He wants to make it easy on his wife. He's willing to do the cheating for both of them.

* * *

Marrying her has all the promise of getting a kidney transplant from a bedwetter.

* * *

She's such a nymphomaniac. She went to the doctor recently and he told her to stay off her back for a few days.

* * *

She has forty-two towels in her hope chest . . . each one from a different hotel.

* * *

He wears a girdle . . . ever since his wife found it in the glove compartment of his car.

118

She's the perfect secretary. She types fast and runs slow.

* * *

He enjoyed *The Art of Sex* so much he didn't put his girlfriend down till he'd finished it.

* * *

She's like a flower. She grows wild in the woods.

* * *

She doesn't mind if a man doesn't fit the bill as long as he foots it.

* * *

She may be good for nothing, but she's never bad for nothing.

* * *

She was a telephone operator for a while and had three close calls.

* * *

It's not easy to become her husband. First of all you have to be listed in the phone book.

She knows where bad little girls go—everywhere!

* * *

His wife had to let the maid go because he wouldn't.

* * *

He's the kind of guy who can change gears in a Volkswagon and not get his face slapped.

* * *

She's the kind of girl half the guys in town want to marry. The other half already has.

* * *

She's fooled around with so many sailors, her lips go in and out with the tide.

* * *

He'd be in great shape if his blood had as much circulation as his wife.

* * *

He and many of his friends used to have sex with the same girl, but he must have been the best man. He married her.

On his honeymoon night he asked his wife if he was the first one. She said she couldn't understand why everybody asked the same question.

* * *

In school she made the band. She also made the football team and anybody else who passed by.

* * *

She's so oversexed her panty hose has an answering service.

* * *

The only time he likes to see a girl stick to her knitting is when she's in a wet bathing suit.

X

P.U.!

His laundry just came back. It was rejected.

People used to turn their noses up at him. Now they hold them.

* * *

Some people say he isn't fit to sleep with pigs. Most people say he is.

* * *

He must have gotten up on the wrong side of the gutter.

* * *

There are people you wouldn't touch with a ten-foot pole. It would be all right to touch him if the pole could be burned afterwards.

* * *

He came from the wrong side of the tracks . . . underneath.

* * *

His mother didn't know much about babies. When he was born, she went out and bought one Pampers.

* * *

His breath is strong enough to start a windmill.

125

She'll never forget the day she took her first bath. Or the day she took her last bath . . . it was the same day.

* * *

He's a real jock. You can tell by his strap.

* * *

He has black hair and nails to match.

* * *

When he cleans his nails he loses twenty pounds.

* * *

He's so dirty he has to wear a Roach Motel around his neck.

* * *

They ought to keep her in the refrigerator to keep her from getting spoiled.

* * *

She reminds people of some TV shows: *Cagney and Lousy. Pukes of Hazzard. Latrine and Shirley.*

He follows the horses . . . with a pail
and a shovel.

He ought to be put in his place. Is there a shovel around?

* * *

She wears a great perfume—Chanel five-and-ten.

* * *

He just came off an onion diet. He lost five pounds and eighteen friends.

* * *

He didn't know she liked onions, but it didn't take long for him to get wind of it.

* * *

He looks like the kind of guy who would come over to your house and crap in your pool.

* * *

He wears turtleneck sweaters . . . to cover his flea collar.

* * *

He has a black belt in crud.

He wears Italian suits. They have hair
under the sleeves.

XI

VICIOUS!
ROTTEN!
CREEP!

She's a sweet girl. She probably wouldn't hurt a lion.

* * *

He's so rotten, he gives wrong directions to an ambulance.

* * *

She's a tough cookie. She's got more balls than a poolroom.

* * *

Does she go to a manicurist or does she do her own claws?

* * *

You can't mention his name without a choking sensation. And that's what most people would like to do to him.

* * *

He's a man of conviction. Several times.

* * *

He's a born crook. They say he's following in his father's fingerprints.

His family used to hang around a lot, especially from trees.

He's so low he can read dice from the bottom.

* * *

The best that can be said about him is that he had four rotten brothers and he was the best of the batch.

* * *

He was connected to the police department. With a pair of handcuffs.

* * *

Her face is her fortune. She should keep it in a vault.

* * *

He's followed the Ten Commandments all of his life. It's a shame he never caught up to them.

* * *

He was born in the hills and hasn't been on the level since.

* * *

He'd murder his parents then beg for mercy because he was an orphan.

He'd steal the teeth out of your mouth and then serve you hard food.

* * *

She's vicious. When she dies she wants to be cremated and thrown in somebody's face.

* * *

Her husband hates her. When she promised to dance on his grave, he decided to be buried at sea.

* * *

At her weddings, they don't have a bridegroom. They have an opponent.

* * *

She begged him to give her eighteen inches and hurt her. So he made love to her six times and rapped her in the mouth.

* * *

She's a real ballbreaker. That's why she's in his last will and testicle.

* * *

Nobody's pinned anything on him since he was a baby.

135

He's so crooked, he has a corkscrew shadow.

* * *

Some people say he's a pain in the back. Others have a lower opinion of him.

* * *

He'd send boxes of mud to hurricane victims.

* * *

His folks hated him so much, they hired another kid to play him in home movies.

* * *

She's a female clone—a clunt.

* * *

She's so tough she was probably a riveter *before* the war.

* * *

She won't go to the beach because she says that the sea air disagrees with her. Her husband doesn't see how it would dare.

136

He's got more nerve than a root canal.

* * *

She ought to take the midnight broom out of town.

* * *

He's the kind of guy who'd like to deliver bad news for the War Department.

* * *

She's the kind of hostess you thank for her hostility.

* * *

He has the disposition of an untipped waiter.

* * *

He has the personality of a traffic cop with heartburn.

* * *

When he was born, something terrible happened . . . he lived.

He's like the Statue of Liberty. He says, "Give me your tired, your poor, your wretched . . . your watch, your money."

*   *   *

Her heart is as pure as the driven slush.

*   *   *

His version of the Golden Rule is simple— Do unto others.

*   *   *

He's like French bread . . . very little dough but lots of crust.

*   *   *

We've all heard the expression, "The worst is yet to come." He just arrived.

*   *   *

He's a man of exact words. When he sees a sign that says "wet floor," he does.

*   *   *

He'd give you a penny for your thoughts and we all know what kind of animal gives a scent.

He acts as if the whole world is against him . . . and it is.

* * *

He ought to go to a Fotomat and get his negative personality developed.

* * *

She has a very even disposition . . . always rotten.

* * *

He's okay as people go, and people wish he would.

* * *

He was the type of kid his mother told him not to play with.

* * *

He stabs more people in the back than sciatica.

* * *

He has knifed more people than a surgeon.

He's so devious, he can stab you in the back from the front.

* * *

Somebody ought to throw him a dinner and hope that it hits him.

* * *

He got a black eye fighting for a girl's honor. Too bad she wanted to keep it.

* * *

You can count his enemies on the fingers of the Mormon Tabernacle Choir.

* * *

He's so crooked that if he swallowed a nail he'd cough up a corkscrew.

* * *

He's a vicious guy. He gives half of his income to piranha research.

* * *

He was so hated he had to be his own buddy at camp.

140

He gives people a certain warmth. Of course you can get the same from a rectal suppository.

* * *

His heart would be great for a transplant. It's never been used.

* * *

He picks his friends . . . to pieces.

* * *

The other day she hit him with a chair. She couldn't lift the table.

* * *

She has a tongue that could clip a hedge.

* * *

People know he likes sex and travel so they tell him to fuck off.

* * *

He's so vicious, Dial-A-Prayer told him to go to hell.

People take an instant dislike to him. They don't want to waste time.

* * *

She was so tough, her vibrator was made by Black & Decker.

* * *

He's the kind of guy who'd take a bugle to a cemetery and blow reveille.

* * *

He doesn't have too many faults but he sure makes the most of those he does have.

* * *

He's not really his own worst enemy—not while anyone else is still around.

* * *

He always holds her hand . . . and twists it until she drops the knife.

* * *

He used to go with a girl who had a wooden leg. One day he got mad and broke it off.

He'd throw a drowning man both ends of a rope.

* * *

He's such a rat, he tells his kids that Santa Claus is too old to get around much anymore.

* * *

He came from a tough neighborhood. The Avon Lady was Rocky.

* * *

He's got a great line, and people wish he'd hang himself with it.

* * *

If you kicked him in the heart you'd break your toe.

* * *

He'd steal a fly from a blind spider.

* * *

He got sore the other day because she threw out his clothes. He was wearing them at the time.

He made the top of the heap and that about covers it.

* * *

He has been asked out by many beautiful women . . . he's in their homes at the time.

* * *

He's so tough, when he gets a blood transfusion it has to be nailed on.

* * *

The other day she threw him out of the house. Of course, they live in a mobile home that was doing seventy at the time.

* * *

He's so mean, if cannibals stewed him they'd just eat the vegetables.

—   * * *

He's so mean, he'd steal the suckle from a piglet.

* * *

He should be an elevator operator. He's always running people down.

He's really a nice guy. Once a day he walks his cobra.

He's so unliked Oral Roberts wouldn't lay a hand on him.

* * *

He's kissed so many asses his lips have hemorrhoids.

* * *

He's so mean, he would have shortsheeted Mahatma Gandhi.

* * *

He's got guts. There's nothing he wouldn't tell you to your face that he wouldn't tell behind your back.

* * *

She's so cold she has arctic circles under her eyes.

XII

TOO FAT!
TOO SKINNY!

Well, he's here in the flesh. And when I say "flesh," I'm speaking loosely.

* * *

She has calves only a mother cow could love.

* * *

Her ass is so big, it has its own heart and lungs.

* * *

Her ass is so big, she could moon Pennsylvania.

* * *

She wanted a baby's skin, but they didn't have one her size.

* * *

She won't go swimming. She's afraid of being harpooned.

* * *

Men look down her dress and compliment her on her shoes.

He's so thin he can pull his shorts on from either end.

* * *

She's never had any trouble walking the straight and narrow. That's because she's so straight and narrow.

* * *

She's so thin, when she swallows an olive ten guys leave town.

* * *

She tries to build up her body. She smears pollen on her chest and prays for bees.

* * *

It isn't what she puts into her dress that's interesting, it's what she leaves out.

* * *

He was so thin he was afraid to go to the poolroom. Every time he walked in, they tried to chalk him.

* * *

She's so fat she won't sit down anymore. She's afraid of high places.

She was so flat-chested, her baby had to nurse with a straw.

She eats so much, she puts mayonnaise on an aspirin.

* * *

She's pretty fat. She has to wear two girdles, an upper and a lower.

* * *

Her Living Bra isn't sure it's worth living.

* * *

She stuffed her bra with Charmin and still nobody squeezed.

* * *

She eats so much, when she dies she wants to be cremated and her ashes put into a dip.

* * *

If it wasn't for her Adam's apple, she wouldn't have any figure at all.

* * *

Her ass isn't what it's cracked up to be.

When he was a baby, his parents folded him in half and left him under a windshield wiper at a shopping mall.

152

She's so fat, they had to let out her garment bag.

* * *

He went on a banana diet. He didn't lose any weight but he loves to swing from trees.

* * *

Her girdle is so tight, every time she opens it she gets three inches taller.

* * *

Science wonders what would happen if you crossed a crocodile and a hippopotamus. He knows because he has her.

* * *

He's not fat. He's just a little broad-shouldered around the belt.

* * *

He started to broaden his mind from his ass up.

* * *

His pants are so tight you can tell his religion.

All her sweater does for her is make her itch.

* * *

She's so skinny, this morning she took a shower and it missed her.

* * *

He's so small he's a waste of skin.

* * *

He has two regrets in his life. He has to wake up to eat and he has to stop eating to sleep.

* * *

As a kid he was so thin, his teacher kept marking him absent.

* * *

He was such a big baby, the doctor was afraid to slap him when he was born.

* * *

She was cute from her head to her foot, but she made a mess of what was in between.

154

She's so fat she could sell shade.

* * *

If she puts on another ten pounds she can become another city.

* * *

It's very hard to lose her in a crowd . . . because she is a crowd.

XIII

VAIN!
AND WHAT AN
EGO!

Every time he looks in the mirror he takes a bow.

* * *

He has carried on a great love affair for a long time . . . unassisted.

* * *

He loves himself so much he has towels marked "His" and "His."

* * *

He's got a big head. Sears wouldn't paint it for $99.95.

* * *

Speaking of girls . . . and he usually is.

* * *

He's wrapped up in himself and he makes a very untidy package.

* * *

He thinks he's so handsome, he once tried to knock himself up.

People have to be careful when they talk about him. They're speaking of the man he loves.

* * *

He's always me-deep in conversation.

* * *

He makes love to himself at night while watching "The Price Is Right."

* * *

If he had his life to live over he would still fall in love with himself.

* * *

He's a self-made man. But he looks more like a warning than an example.

* * *

She holds her nose so high she has a double chin at the back of her neck.

* * *

He's got a terrible inferiority complex. He just met somebody as good as he is.

159

Her hair turned gray while she worried about being a blonde or a brunette.

* * *

He's the kind of guy who starts the bull rolling.

XIV

BONUSES:
CRACKS FOR
ALL OCCASIONS.

I don't know what I'd do without you. But I'd rather.

* * *

We don't know what we'd do without you, but it's worth a try.

* * *

He must get very tired of having himself around.

* * *

Next time he passes your house, be grateful.

* * *

X-rays couldn't tell what people see in him.

* * *

Why don't you go for a long walk on a short pier?

* * *

His father should go back to the beginning of his seven-year itch and start from scratch.

People worship the ground her father left her.

* * *

The poor girl spent six months trying to find herself. When she did, it wasn't her.

* * *

A man's a fool to marry a woman, but what else can he marry?

* * *

Without her he'd never be where he is today . . . broke.

* * *

One day he'll learn that it's only a matter of about eighteen inches between a pat on the back and a kick in the pants.

* * *

Absence makes the heart grow fonder, and everybody'd like to love him.

* * *

His parents were too poor to have children. A neighbor had him.

163

He has a diary of all their good times together. It's called a checkbook.

* * *

When her mother asked her father to change the baby, he wasn't sure they'd give him another kid.

* * *

He's a panhandler—an intern at a hospital.

* * *

She's a cancan girl: "Can I have a car? Can I have a coat? Can I have a diamond?"

* * *

She brings out the animal in men . . . mink.

* * *

One day he asked her for her hand . . . and it's been in his pocket ever since.

* * *

He's so withdrawn, he won't even look a potato in the eye.

164

He's the eternal optimist. He keeps waiting for a Truman Capote Junior.

* * *

She doesn't care if you're a cad . . . as long as you own one.

* * *

He remembers the day they met. He opened his wallet and there she was.

* * *

She dresses to kill and cooks the same way.

* * *

He keeps blowing his horn, but that's because he's in a fog.

* * *

He was having oral sex with this girl for three hours. Unfortunately, the last two hours she spent running for a bus.

* * *

She found the wolf at her door, but one day she invited him in for dinner and he starved to death.

He never tells his wife anything. His neighbors do it for him.

* * *

She's so short her miniskirt drags on the floor.

* * *

We've all heard of mouth-to-mouth resuscitation and artificial insemination. He practices mouth-to-mouth insemination.

* * *

The other day he proposed to her. She was so surprised she fell out of bed.

* * *

She was a brunette, but she went to a gambling casino, got into a crap game, and faded, faded, faded.

* * *

He had a lot of get up and go. Most people wished that he would.

* * *

He's vain. Instead of glasses, he has a prescription windshield.

166

He was determined to climb the ladder of success. He's not a success but he can sure climb ladders.

* * *

She believes that a ring on her finger is worth two on the phone.

* * *

He picked her the same way an apple picks a farmer.

* * *

His conscience hurts him when everything else feels good.

* * *

He was so lonely without her, it was almost like having her there.

* * *

She has the skin of a ten-year-old, but she's getting it awfully wrinkled.

* * *

He has a lot of women eating out of his hand. He's a waiter.

His bath toys should have been a toaster and a radio.

Some women won't get married till they're twenty-five. She won't be twenty-five till she gets married.

* * *

He broke his nose the other day. His boss stopped short.

* * *

One day she got so angry with him, she took off her engagement ring and flung it on to her other hand.

* * *

She's got the kind of look that hangs a price tag on every object in the room.

* * *

He takes a look at a girl and he knows what kind of past she's going to have.

* * *

He's of Italian extraction. He once pulled out of a hooker in Rome.

* * *

He's a hypochondriac. Every time he sneezes he cures a dozen people.

He was a little Greek boy, but he left
home. He didn't like the way he was being
reared.

Of all his relations he likes sex the best.

* * *

She's interested in do, re, mi and she's going fa.

* * *

Keeping a secret from her is like trying to sneak daybreak past a rooster.

* * *

She refused to marry this elderly millionaire. She dreaded the thought of old age creeping up on her.

* * *

He's got so much money he could commit suicide jumping off his wallet.

* * *

He has the manners of a gentleman. He ought to return them.

* * *

He could be a distant relative . . . and the further the better.

People wonder what makes him tick. Most would like it to be a time bomb.

* * *

She's a great driver. She gets forty miles to a fender.

* * *

He comes from a dry town in the Midwest. There are fish there who still haven't learned to swim.

* * *

If he wasn't crazy, he'd go nuts.

* * *

He's slightly effeminate. In school he starred in a production of *Queen Lear*.

* * *

She won't go anywhere without her mother . . . and her mother will go anywhere.

* * *

On his way home he ought to jaywalk.

Her father said that the man who married her would get a prize. He married her and he's still waiting for the prize.

* * *

She's a preacher's daughter, but nobody can put anything pastor.

* * *

. They must have found him in the bottom drawer at the Bureau of Missing Persons.

* * *

He was really the active sort. He would move more in a week than most people do in an hour.

* * *

People keep pulling her leg. They're trying to even it up with the other one.

* * *

She's very emotional. She cries when a traffic light is against her.

* * *

Her jeans are so tight, she has to carry her hanky in her mouth.

She has a lovely diamond. What did it cost? Her?

* * *

Why doesn't he leave and let live?

* * *

She's very strange with a checkbook. Once she's started one, she can't put it down until she's finished.

* * *

He's very shy. He can't open an oyster without first knocking on the shell.

* * *

He's so tense, he twangs in a high wind.

* * *

He was abroad for ten years and still walks like it.

* * *

She had hazel eyes, chestnut hair, almond skin . . . she was nuts.

He's not effeminate, he just walks with a lisp.

*　*　*

We'll make him eat his words . . . as soon as he gets teeth.

*　*　*

Let's have nothing out of you but breathing. And very little of that.

*　*　*

God made man and then he rested. Then he made woman, and since then nobody's rested.

*　*　*

She's a regular Cinderella. You have to slipper ten, you have to slipper twenty.

*　*　*

He ran away from home when he was a kid, and they never found him. They never looked for him.

He has a list of girls as long as his arm. But who wants to go out with girls as long as his arm?

* * *

He's such a coward, he entered the army as a P.O.W.

* * *

She'll get along well. She knows how to play piano, tennis . . . and dumb.

* * *

He dreamed of a vine-covered cottage with little things crawling on the floor. And he wanted children too.

* * *

Ten years ago he had thick wavy hair. Now the waves are gone and there's nothing but beach.

* * *

He's not choosy. He likes her for what she is—rich!

He's descended from a long line his mother listened to.

*   *   *

She's always wanted to have soft white skin—ermine.

*   *   *

One day somebody gave her a gift certificate. She exchanged it.

*   *   *

She took it so hard when she hit forty that she bounced right back to thirty-five.

*   *   *

He lives in the part of town where people's dogs come from a better family than he does.

*   *   *

When he was born, his father tried to collect on his accident insurance.

*   *   *

He spent his whole life behind the eight ball. His mother liked to shoot pool.

He must have bought that outfit by accident. It fits him like a bandage.

* * *

On Halloween, they dress him up as a speed bump.

* * *

He doesn't trust anybody. He makes his shadow walk in front of him.

* * *

She's the kind of girl who can cure men of whistling.

* * *

She's been married so many times, she's got rice marks.

* * *

She comes from a family of long livers. Two days after her grandmother died, they had to beat her liver to death with a stick.

* * *

He's got a golden tongue. He can convince his wife she looks bad in mink.

He said he worked in a place with four hundred people under him. He's a guard in a cemetery.

He's got the nerve of two porcupines making love.

* * *

He's been washing his hair too much. It's shrinking.

* * *

His suit fits him like a glove. He ought to get one that fits him like a suit.

* * *

In his school they had a recess every half-hour . . . to carry out the wounded.

* * *

He's so unlucky, if he sawed a woman in half he'd get the part that eats.

* * *

He never knew what real happiness was until they met. Now it's too late.

* * *

The doctor told him to take iron pills. They worked until he got caught in the rain and turned into rust.

He used to eat dehydrated food right out of the package. One time he got caught in the rain and put on a hundred and sixty pounds.

* * *

She's always making salmon for him. Three times a week, salmon. When spring comes, he gets the urge to go north to spawn.

* * *

Why doesn't he go down to the ocean and pull a wave over his head?!

* * *

He told her he'd die if she turned him down. She did and sixty-two years later he died.

* * *

His parents were so poor they couldn't afford talcum powder. For two years he had to rough it.

* * *

He's so bald, Warren Beatty has more hair on his lapel.

She has affectionate knees. You can't keep them apart.

* * *

He brings out a lot in others. He makes them throw up.

* * *

He knows the exact minute he's going to die. A judge just told him.

* * *

They're unemployed schoolteachers. One has no class and the other has no principal.

* * *

He was a precocious child. When he was four months old he was already eating solids . . . pencils, crayons, books.

* * *

He had a terrible accident recently. He had the right of way but the other guy had the truck.

ABOUT THE AUTHOR

A well-known television writer, Milt Rosen is also the author of eight books that sold well in his house. His latest book on the repair and maintenance of meter maids has been bought by a major studio as a vehicle for Mother Theresa and Richard Pryor. Another of his books on the training of garden snails will be turned into a sixteen-hour mini-series on NBC.

Milt has a young wife with whom he has had sex as recently as 1978, four children who range in age from rotten to detestable, two dogs, and a mortgage the size of Siberia.

As mean as many of the jokes in this compilation are, Milt can be found in drafts raising obscene goose bumps for Braille perverts.